Scotch Tape World

Poems

Tom C. Hunley

Accents Publishing • Lexington KY • 2013

Copyright © 2013 by Tom C. Hunley
All rights reserved

Printed in the United States of America

Accents Publishing
Editor: Katerina Stoykova-Klemer
Cover Design: Simeon Kondev
Cover Image: *Couples performing underwater at Weeki Wachee Springs near Brooksville* Courtesy of State Library and Archives of Florida

Accents Publishing is an independent press for brilliant voices.
For a catalog of current and upcoming titles, please visit us on the Web at http://www.accents-publishing.com

ISBN: 978-1-936628-20-9
First Edition

For Ralaina

Contents

Um / 1
Permanent / 2
Wives of the Poets / 4
Psalm on a Theme by Dean Young and a Somewhat Similar
    Theme by Allen Ginsberg / 6
At the Afterlife Bar and Grill / 8
Self-Portrait as a Child's Stick Figure Drawing
    on a Refrigerator / 9
Road Test / 10
Another Dream of Falling / 12
Turning Yourself into the Wind / 13
Elegy/Litany / 14
Confessions of a Failed Beatnik / 16
VC / 19
No One to Ask for Directions / 20
Inside the Belly / 21
While We Were on Fire,
    Our Shadows Glided on Water / 22
Thaw / 24
Death and Other Dirty Jokes / 25
Scotch Tape World / 27
Paranoid Love Song / 29
P.S. and P.P.S. / 30

Acknowledgments / 33

Um

Often I'm awakened by awful noises,
jackhammers, dynamite, walls crumbling
and bigger ones climbing the sky
in their places. My future arrives and I
have to settle for it. I don't understand how
I got here any more than a lobster understands
how it ended up in a tank next to a *Please wait
to be seated* sign, but both of us can read
the faces of the cruelly beautiful women
pointing at us. I always feel eyes on me,
so I apologize to insects after I kill them
and to the salmon on my plate, caught
being nostalgic for home. Everything makes sense
if you squint just right, and at least once a day
I realize that whatever I've been saying
isn't the point at all. I spend most days listening
to other people almost making sense, and I don't
ask them what the hell they're talking about
because they're on television or the radio, or
because I'm eavesdropping from the next table.
When I'm not talking or listening, I'm in a
boil, my shell softening. I'm getting a good look
at a wrecking ball. I'm crumbling.
I volunteered for all this, accidentally,
by raising my hand, intending to ask
a question I couldn't put into words.

Permanent

Hey, your tattoo fell off, I said, and picked it up,
but she thought I was trying to pick her up,
so she rushed away, her legs long and tan except
for a balloon-shaped vacancy on her ankle where
the tattoo had rented space. She was beautiful with
curly hair and probably men had been hitting on her
for as long as she could remember, and maybe she
assumed that fending off their attentions would be
a permanent part of her life. Listen, my parents died
last year. They were always there, hovering,
when I was small. First the air went out
of their marriage, and then Pop was gone, and after that,
Mom was gone, and a little while after that, I made up
that preposterous story about the woman whose tattoo
fell off, I guess to illustrate something about impermanence.
I should have just said that in Seattle, circa 1991, I saw
a Blood or maybe a Crip with a tattoo of a tear under
his eye. Since then, the Bloods and Crips have gone legit.
They own their own record labels, plus a nightclub or two
in Rainier Valley and a majority share in Tully's Coffee.
A work crew dynamited the Kingdome in 2000,
and Mt. Rainier is an active volcano, so even it
won't stand forever, and I haven't lived
in my hometown for fifteen years, but that woman
I started to tell you about, she poured her whole self
into an embrace with this scuzzball of my acquaintance.
Good woman finds bad man and gets lost.
That theme is a fixture on Lifetime and Oxygen.
I shouldn't have made that up about my parents dying
or about the gangs trafficking in coffee. I wanted,
I guess, to show you something about impermanence.
I wanted, ironically, to make a lasting impression
on the subject. I should have just led with the fact
that the old Rainier Brewery is now the headquarters
for Tully's Coffee. If a landmark like that can't last,
maybe no one's marriage has a chance; maybe all of us

should tattoo tears beneath our eyes or fill our hearts
with helium and reckless love and let them fly
untethered and brightly-colored across the sky.

Wives of the Poets

Last week I told my class how Elinor Frost never forgave Robert
for little Elliot's death. She thought he didn't alert medics fast
    enough.
"Maybe he took the road with too much traffic,"
cracked a bearded, bespectacled young man,
"or got lost in the beauty of the woods."
"How can you joke about them losing a child?"
accused a young woman with long earrings and boots,
and we launched into "Home Burial."

Flip a shiny quarter and it's either an eagle
flying away as fast as it can or a dead president
trying to look dignified despite the worms
under his wig. This week I tell them
Wallace Stevens said "A poet looks at the world
the way a man looks at a woman," but he
and his wife, Elsie, lived in separate sections of their house
and he never wrote her a love poem.
"Thirteen ways of looking at a jackass,"
murmurs the young woman, arms and brows crossed,
and the young man replies, "I'll bet he got tired of her
getting on his case when he just wanted to unwind
with a little Guitar Hero," and I say, "We don't know
much about his life, but…"

It's fall semester, and as the trees bare themselves, the students
cover up and take back all the promises of spring
as the hot kisses they've planted on each other
ice over, and I know that next week when I tell them about
Williams Carlos Williams cheating on his wife, Flossie, these
    two
will say, "So much depends upon you flirting with my
    roommate,"
and "Not ideas about the cheapskate but the cheapskate
    himself."

Today you broke the garage door and said "I'm sorry."
You let the laundry pile up, and you're sorry.
Here I am airing our dirty laundry. I'm sorry,
you married a writer. All day I've planned my classes
and now I'm far away from you, lost in the woods of this poem,
which isn't great or maybe even good, and I'm sorry
that literary biographers and classrooms in the future
probably won't be discussing our marriage.
We're a sorry couple and no longer young,
but flip a coin a hundred times, and fifty times you'll forgive me,
and fifty times I'll tell you there's nothing to forgive.

Psalm on a Theme by Dean Young and a Somewhat Similar Theme by Allen Ginsberg

When I die, Lord, I want to come back
as a cloud an airplane passes through
just before the crash,
lit up by blazing sunset
and just freed of a heavy, cleansing rain—
a cloud gifted with speech
enough to say *Change your course, pilot.*
I want to change, cloudlike,
into the sort of person who finds a wallet
and an abandoned infant and knows which to keep,
which to return, and does it. Sometimes I lose myself
in a crowd. Sometimes I find myself
in a cloud. Sometimes I want to die, Lord,
from embarrassment. An expression
like *I'm falling apart* or *I love you to pieces,*
but if I do fall apart, Lord, I do
want you to love me to pieces.
It is written in a Dean Young poem,
The mind is a tiny island you've washed upon.
Is that true, Lord? About me, not you, I mean.
Dean Young the poet, not Dean Young the creator
of the comic strip, *Blondie*, I mean.
Allen Ginsberg wrote, *I'm sick of my own mind.*
Give me just a little piece of yours, Lord.
I'm going to give you a piece of my mind
is an expression, but I mean it literally.
I feel like a sandwich is an expression
meaning I crave bread and cheese
with ham/lettuce/mustard if you please,
but sometimes I do feel like Dagwood has
his eyes then his hands then his drooling mouth on me
and I feel like I know how Blondie must feel.
This makes me realize I don't want to die.

I've wandered forty years through the desert
of my mind, Lord. I want you to fill my mouth
with water and prayer and maybe a jagged little song.

At the Afterlife Bar and Grill

A glass falls and fills the clouds with shards,
a broken window with that old blue and green marble
on the other side, magnified so we almost think
we can go back. A kitten mewing in a woodpile.
A child lost on the street. A mother, panicked
at the police station, her lucky penny tossed
down the wrong well. We can't do anything
but watch and maybe, finally, get to know
our neighbors. The world was Eden after all,
but after dark, before fire. We never could see
the great Godzilla, but something smelled awful
and our friends kept getting stepped on.
Over a drink, we remember cold nights that froze
our beards. Over another, we recall how sharing
a cigarette was the closest we got most nights to sharing
each other's breath. The silliness of believing
that sleep and wakefulness were different states.
That *I love you* and *fuck off* were antonyms.
Our talk flows like the mighty Mississippi.
Alive, we could never find the right words,
blind dates who said they'd come right back but didn't.
The barmaid's an angel, and the low yowl of Mozart
and Mingus's latest jam rises from the juke box
like a body from a tomb. *Alive, I was a radio
that lost reception*, I say. *There were miracles
everywhere*, I say, *on earth as it is in heaven,
but my eyes were union workers on their lunch break.*
These hot wings are miracles, but everything's a miracle.
You say, *let me tell you something in confidence.*
Your voice climbs onto some ledge
that my ears can't walk you off of.
You say *I can't handle all these miracles.*
You drink until you fall down because
it's way too much for you to stand.

Self-Portrait as a Child's Stick Figure Drawing on a Refrigerator

> *"You are not what you think you are. You are something to be imagined."*
> —Clayton Eshleman

Often I'm a musical instrument
that's afraid of the sounds inside.
My days consist of arrayed efforts
not to hear or hum.
I'm like a baby who screams
at first seeing his arms swinging,
unaware those whips flung
straight at his head are attached to his body.
Why are you doing this to me?
a man asks his body as it fights sleep
and the crucial appendage droops after a woman
says *okay, why not*, after steak and lobster
and Sandra Bullock's latest formulaic schlock.
So spent, his body mocks him; he can't
fathom how he ever lifted the long-stemmed rose
he gave her, now drooping a little bit, too.
In my son's latest drawing labeled "Daddy,"
my hairs are stray spaghetti strands,
my head an oversized triangle crushing my stick-thin frame,
and a briefcase weighs down my three-fingered hand.
Often I feel sketchy like that, as if all the wrong colors
spill over my faint lines and anyone could cross me out
just like that. I haven't always felt like a stick figure.
I haven't always been an instrument
left forgotten in its case. I remember a time
in junior high when Doug Dickerson passed me
a pornographic flip book, the male stick figure's stick penis
getting bigger and bigger and the female stick figure's
stick legs getting farther and farther apart
until the stick figure bed broke and something hidden
deep inside me broke out, broke my body wide open,
a strange inchoate music that wanted to come out.

Road Test

1. Two roads diverged in a yellow wood. What did you do?
   a. I recited Robert Frost until one road lit up like my neighbor's house at Christmas time, then I took the darker road to spite my neighbor, who borrowed and never returned my rake, and that has made all the difference
   b. I picked the winding road, and I Kerouaced across it, Jack, oh didn't I, Daddy-O
   c. I imagined what it must feel like to be the road, rain and sun taking turns slapping it, the lonely odor of roadkill, the ability to touch origin and destination all at once, like some crushingly-sad superhero
   d. I did what my GPS told me to do

2. What signs did you see along the way?
   a. Hell is Real! on my left, Adult Books and Videos on my right, and the turn I took has made all of the difference
   b. Washington DC or bust (in my rear view mirror, in my dust)
   c. just the clouds, cumulus and blueblack, but with a thread of sunlight, a golden hook at the end
   d. all of the above

3. Did the road turn on you, darkened, pot-holed, a road like Cormac McCarthy's, the sun peeling the clothes off your skin and the skin off your bones?
   a. Yes. I died with this song on my lips
   b. Yes. I offered my bones to the vultures, quoting Robinson Jeffers: "What an enskyment! What a life after death."
   c. No, but some bandits beat me, left me for a corpse. Some folks from my hometown just walked on by, and now there's weirdness when I see them at Starbucks or Lowe's. Someone from the next town over stopped, called 9-1-1 for me, even visited me at the hospital, so

now I don't know how to root when our high school football teams clash
d. No, I still have my clothes and my skin—and that has made all of the difference

4. What did you find at the end of the road?
    a. another road, another wood, another thrill-ride for my screaming blood
    b. just another false wizard who failed me
    c. no pot of gold, just some worthless mutual funds and T-bills
    d. I'd like to say I found myself, I found love, I found God, but I've found that to get there—to get anywhere—you've got to veer far away from the straight yellow line, the paved path; you've got to make your own road and be ready to crash.

Another Dream of Falling

Potato chip-colored old man, I don't know you
or where you pedaled your bicycle as I
drove by, just as birds don't know anything
of the pockets of air they fly past. We were
on Main Street in Osage, Iowa. I was driving
to see a dying relative for the last time. You
were thin and bald, and in your green windbreaker
you reminded me of a turtle. Driving on was like
turning a page and watching one story become
another. Outside Sioux Falls I saw a white car
so dirt-packed I couldn't read the license plate,
the way I can't tell time in my sleep. Later I saw
some cows lazing in front of a "Wear Fur" sign.
I forgot my name and wished I knew yours
as the sun hit the pavement before setting.
I slept in a hotel bed and dreamed of flying
and then falling beneath the sound of my own breathing.
I dreamed of the broad curves of Crazy Woman
Creek Road, which I had driven down days before
as the sky hazed over. I dreamed of dying
but it was like a turtle entering water, the water
creasing and then smoothing itself out. Your eyes
had met mine for a second, and I could have sworn
that something passed between us, as if you
tossed a skipping stone through my window
and it landed flat in my hand.

Turning Yourself into the Wind

I know you feel like no one
knows you. I understand
the long, disembodied slide
into the self followed by the urge
to set off car alarms and toss
a garbage lid into the street.
The good news is you're coming together
like those leaves swirling in a column
and then forming a neat mound.
But you still feel invisible, don't you?
You're still the lone citizen
of your own ravenous body.
There you go, chasing after the parts of yourself
you've felt but never found. The bad news is
that they've been watching you, the weathermen,
making their dire predictions, and now they're warning
your neighbors to hide in their basements
or crouch in a ditch somewhere,
waiting it out while you rampage and rage.
Wouldn't it feel better to turn into music
or at least into words?

Elegy/Litany

If I describe the wind as pickpocket subtle
or as a ghost running naked through our yard,
that's called anemographia, but knowing this
won't fill my pockets or scare off the ghosts
that haunt me when the hum of our refrigerator
wakes me up. Having my office computer stolen
woke me up to the need to always back up
files, but I'd rather move forward. In the foreword
to a book on the Mayans, I read that our superstition
of tossing pennies into wells for good luck
has its origins in the Mayan custom of wedding virgins
to the spirit of the Well of Sacrifice. Well.
At least I'm not a lost virgin ghost, unveiled
for some ugly well-spirit. Last week at a $27/night hotel,
I stared at the "continental breakfast,"
one banana muffin covered by a cloud of gnats.
I grimaced, and another hotel guest ate it, saying
"These bugs won't hurt you." All week,
his bearded bug-eating face has haunted me.
The fear of beards is called pogonophobia.
Knowing this won't bring my laptop back
or make you love me any more. This is an elegy
for my lost computer, but it's also an ode
to the way you can mend me with a smile or a kiss.
At Sewanee, I heard Robert Hass say all poems are either
laments, songs about ways to escape a power that can kill us,
or litanies, prayers to a power that can make us feel more alive,
and at the time, I thought that was way too reductive,
but this poem is both. It's impossible
to put out a fire before it's been set, impossible
to scan the hard drive of my mind and eliminate
the virus that threatens to kill my memory,
impossible to save those sacrificed Mayan virgins
or say the right thing every time.
Now I can shop for a new computer. I can
become a Luddite. I can toss myself down a well.

But all I want to do is tell you that every love song,
every romantic movie, makes me think of you,
and no matter which way the wind blows,
it will always carry me back to you.

Confessions of a Failed Beatnik

I'll admit that I shaved my scruff, patched my jeans
and then bought slacks, and what's more, a double-breasted
    suit
and even shoes! matching, polished, and thus disguised,
I followed a trail of perfume that led, like a floral fluting
Pied Piper, out of the Village, out of Manhattan even,
all the way to suburban Kentucky where I lost

myself, Man, where I forgot the words to every song
I'd ever sung to myself, let my dreams come unstitched,
Jack, quit drinking myself into nowhere Zen
stupors, and most afternoons, though not hungover,
I'm so headachy from meetings and emails
that I drive right past the brandy-colored light of

just-before sunset without pulling over to take it in,
then later, rather than watching moonlight
illuminate the wind combing through unmown bluegrass,
I'm wiping kid-puke, there-there, I'm shining a flashlight
on the no-monsters under their bunk bed. I saw
the best minds of my generation toss aside their

necessary suffering, lose the art of losing, trade it all in
for golf clubs, I saw them trade the too-beautiful intensity
of feeling, feeling, feeling, for the calm comfort of
the girl-next-door's bare arms, and I'll admit I sold out, too,
and of late, no one has thought to compare me to a roman
    candle
exploding spider-like while everyone goes "awwww!" No, far
    from it,

in fact, I mean dig this: one Fourth of July afternoon—not
    night—
I seared my foot on a sparkler, oh didn't I, the moral being
don't wear sandals around any kind of lit fireworks, but
my kids were in an excited hurry so I did just that, and when

I showed them how to twirl the fiery wire, a spark landed
right underneath a strap and by the time I de-sandaled, my skin

was oozing fluids, but oh listen Cats, my left hand didn't know
what my right hand was handing it when it offered a handshake
that turned out to be really a handcuff, yes I'll admit I put all
my pot pipes and tricyclics in a box, a mildewed cardboard box
I left in front of my mortgaged tract house with "Free" written
on the side in a pungent, licorice-smelling permanent ink
    smear,

and I'll be the first to admit that I'm not free, that I'll change
two diapers in the time it takes you to read this, that no
odor-proof pail will keep that stench from clinging
to my memory like tobacco to clothes at a dingy tavern,
Daddy-O, and I have to admit that I rarely visit dingy taverns
because my wife hates that smell and she makes me shower

afterwards, so standing here clean-shaven and cologned
and certifiably a carpooler and little-league coach, I hereby
    admit,
Angels, that I disgust myself, not like Robert Lowell as Peeping
    Tom
in "Skunk Hour" but more like a Benedict Arnold of Hiptown
turned double dealing traitor, citizen of Nowheresville. No need
    to point
fingers or a gun to my head, Doves, I'll freely admit that most
    full moons

I don't howl or chase cars, because I have to work the next
    morning,
and I'm not the kind of cat who wears women's underwear,
I've never leapt off a bridge, put my head in an oven,
attended a bullfight, shot my wife in the head while aiming
for an apple, carved my skin and called it research,
gone to prison (except to teach a poetry class), hitched cross

country, stepped in front of a car or tank or dune buggy,
fronted a rock band, or run for office just to write about it.

I don't even keep a bride on the side or any dark secrets
except those of my friends, most of whom are characters
in forgotten novels, and because this is a confessional poem
I'll admit that I'm pee-your-pants scared of my kids.

I mean like they pretend to be ghosts, and I pretend to be
    scared,
right? But I really am scared, pretending not to be.
Scared they'll grow up to be like me in all the wrong ways.
Scared I'll run out of bread and they'll wear secondhand
sweaters, not bohemian chic tatters but real honest-to-Buddha
hand-to-mouth sleeping-on-storm-grates poor. Scared they
    won't

grow up. Scared they'll grow up and I'll grow old, quick as
a car crash, and my poems will be totaled. Scared they'll turn
me into a piano, out of tune, dust on every key.

VC

I just tripped on bamboo in Trung's backyard.
It snapped, not too loud, but loud enough
for him to catch me. We're eleven, playing "VC"
with his four brothers. VC is like Tag,
but if you're "it," you have to pretend
to be the Viet Cong. It's my turn
to be the Viet Cong, but first Trung wants
to tell me something broken and jungledark.
His brothers' laughter betrays their hiding places.
I don't have the heart to find them.

Trung tells me about his sister wailing,
looking back home, looking ready to turn into salt;
about their father's slap on her cheek
followed by a caress on the red spot.
The seasick boat rocks and awaits them.
The latenight air is chilly.

Half of Trung's brothers have peed themselves.
I'm the Viet Cong, and I can almost smell it.
Ten years later, Trung and I smoke some strong
stinky weed together on break from our different
colleges, and I lose him in the haze. I look
on Facebook and in the phone book.
I'll never find him.

No One to Ask for Directions

Do those patches of forest
untouched by man
ever get lonely or
lost inside themselves
with no notion of maps,
no one to ask for directions?
Snow-covered ground no one
ever sees can do anything it wants.
The sun will never know.
There is snow no one notices
and us, melting snowmen
trying to keep the pipes in our mouths
and the organic noses on our faces,
trying to hold it all in.

Inside the Belly

When the light strikes your face
at just the right angle, I can almost
see our future, all bright
and shiny in your eyes
is something I heard Mike say
five times in the same evening
to different women with the same
results, is the first verse of a song
I heard on my car stereo
in a dream I was having about
a road trip past the cornfields
of Indiana. I don't know
anyone named Mike, but I hope
he finally made it, found happiness,
grew into his body, which was clumsy
and slow like a John Deere tractor
bringing traffic to a grinding halt
is the beginning of a story I never
finished reading. Do you believe
there are angels whose whole job
is to salvage all the fragments,
all our half-finished efforts?
Where was I? Oh right, Indiana.
It swallowed me up because I said
I'll be damned before I move to Kentucky
is something I heard a preacher say
while he lassoed a snake above his head.
Something I ate had poisoned me.
I was starting to feel it. My stomach
testified, and a perfumed woman in
a large straw hat shouted Amen.

While We Were on Fire,
Our Shadows Glided on Water

The flames were not literal, though they
embraced like passionate drunken lovers.
We could love one another right
were it not for the pain, the throbbing pain
so strong that even saying your name
makes me want to dive deep into myself,
my cool safe shadow. It's not our fault
that we're made of twigs is the sort
of comment that made many of my dates
turn into jellyfish instead of jelly
and so I learned that yelling "Fire"
too soon can kill a spark. Sometimes
my life alone resembled a mountain,
not in majestic beauty but in its ability
to freeze me to death. Sometimes I get
lost in myself as in Kafka's novels,
but love is a beast that can take any form.
Somehow I keep winding up on its back
and it carries me to you. I didn't know
how alone I could feel until an airplane
put 3,000 miles between us. I thought this
poem was about love but fire, water, it's about
death, about which I know even less.
Death took the poet Jack Gilbert this week,
I know that. I sat in on a couple of his classes,
caught a couple of his readings. He expressed
strong opinions: fans of classical music
lacked passion, tin-hearted semioticians
were stealing young minds. He had his
graduate students write essays about the poems
of Linda Gregg, his former lover, then mailed them
to her. A guy I used to get high with
once got drunk and smashed his knee
with a hammer, on purpose, then hobbled
into a Kroger's, knocked over a shelf,

on purpose, the purpose being to sue them.
He later vanished like April snow, and I received
the funeral announcement a week too late.
My neighbors have been putting up signs
depicting their lost cat, so she is sort of famous.
Fear flashes through their eyes, and sadness.
We're never alone. Our pet worries keep us company.
I have more worries than I have words for them,
but mostly I worry that I'll lose you and wander
around my dark, cluttered self without a cat's night vision.
Jack Gilbert wrote poems about carrying
his grief over the death of Michiko, another lover,
about finding locks of her hair weeks after
the funeral. I thought this poem was about death
but it's about separation, those three weeks last summer
spent across the ocean from you, how I feared
that the distance would kill me.

Thaw

I'm hungry, I told the frozen pizza,
and to the windstorm I said,
*You're from Chicago? My friend
moved there to avoid herself*, which
I can understand, though mostly I'm
speeding towards myself
hoping only to avoid a collision.
I have felt like a furniture sale where
everything must go, you know, before
the arson, and also like the droopy flower
that ruined the whole arrangement
and made the bride cry. I've seen pigeons
staggering in shadows cast by pine trees,
and I've seen drunks ambulating
towards bathrooms in taverns pitch black
except for the lamps above pool tables.
I try to hang on as long as I can,
like the icicles hanging onto office awnings
above the heads of smokers. I've felt at times
like a balloon running out of helium, a car
running out of gas, a pizza box emptied of all
but the crusts. And now, early in my
forty-second February, I feel like
a snowman, as if tomorrow I'll be nothing
but a carrot, a pipe, and ashes where two
charcoal eyes sat before somebody squirted them
with lighter fuel and struck a match.

Death and Other Dirty Jokes

For years I went to AA meetings and told the same
stories, puffed-up with streetwise bravado:
the time I sat on a departing city bus and watched
through the window while my drug dealer was
held up at knife point, the time I woke up shirtless

on a stranger's lawn, the time I drunk-dialed
the previous night's first date from the steel-barred
city drunk tank. None of these stories were lies,
but, as Melville wrote in *Billy Budd*, "Truth
uncompromisingly told, will always have its

ragged edges," and my ragged truth was so much
more pathetic and dull: walking for miles in
Seattle rain without bus fare, collecting beer bottles
in my sister's basement, missing class and giving
the same old excuses, hollow as worn-out jokes

that weren't funny in the first place, like the one
about growing up so poor my mama cut holes
in my pockets so I'd have something to play with.
I repeated that groaner over and over to my eye-rolling
wife, not knowing where I'd first heard it, until

my uncle—whom I hadn't seen for thirty years—
told it at my grandpa's funeral. Those wasted years,
I like to think I was a forgotten Stratocaster trapped in its case,
but in truth, I think I was Esau, unable to see
past the edges of my hunger and the steaming bowl

of stew. I was a stupid kid, eager to toss away his life.
Grandpa, I barely knew you. I know you hand-crafted clocks,
worked for Standard Oil for like forty years, and loved
your 1960 Studebaker. I'm pretty sure you never
wore makeup outside of the coffin. I know you

got old, and now I want to know what that's like. Tell me,
have you heard any good jokes lately? Tell me about
those last coughing fits, the fight to keep your soul
from bursting out of your body like a blurt or a fart.
Tell me something crude and coarse and side-splitting true.

Scotch Tape World

Taping my thigh and calf together
at the knee, I contemplate taking
my children to Scotch Tape World,
where stars fall from the sky
like posters from my office door, where
the tires could fly off our car at
any moment. It's time they learn
that life is like that, that Disney lies
in the way of a true education. God
never lies, but He's still in trouble.
Why else would He have to clean
all the blackboards on which we
are math problems and incorrect sums?
Our prayers go to Heaven, but first they go
through Scotch Tape World. Torn in transport,
they're pieced back together and presented
to God, who receives them as music
rather than as words. Holding your breath
waiting for people to be decent is one way
to go to God, who loves us just as He loves
the notes that David's harp wrote to Him.
Low clouds overhead seem to come
apart as if held together by cheap Scotch
Tape. Such a pointless death, like the one
suffered by my first car, not to mention
Kenneth Patchen, who wrote "The animal
I wanted couldn't get into the world" and
other lines penned, as Valery said, "by someone
other than the poet to someone other than
the reader." Our prayers might be missives
from someone other than us to someone
other than God. Behind my beard is a face
that's different from the one my wife fell in
love with years ago. Behind any given joke
is the funk that made us look for
laughter. If you don't know what I mean,

you'll wake up one day knowing. You'll
look up and see sunlight hitting a mountain
so hard they both seem ready to shatter.

Paranoid Love Song

As if I've never seen you smile at my
friends right in front of my face, which I
straightened with all my strength.
As if I weren't receiving daily phone calls
from my future self warning me of potholes
that I step in anyway because how do I know
my future self isn't fucking with me?
I know myself, and it's the kind of thing
I'd do. As if I could be king and you
could be queen, which David Bowie promised
but did he mean you and me?
Who's been calling your cell, verse one.
Your hand on my best friend's knee,
come on and admit it, verse two.
As if I say all this to you and you say
as if. As if I was a werewolf but now
I'm Scott again, and I say *I'm sorry
I about bit your head off back there.*
As if I could become your pet parrot and call
your new boyfriend *Cracker*, his penis *peanut*.
As if my heart darkened and you opened
the window blinds to make a sunlight square
to soak it in. As if you would ever leave me
for Richard Dawson. He kisses every female
Family Feud contestant. When I close my eyes
all I see are fruit flies. When they close their eyes
all they see is garbage. The garbage truck comes
with screeching brakes while they're sleeping
and they wake bereft. Buzzing and banging heads
against screen doors. Like me after the inevitable
bull comes charging at me. After you've left.

P.S. and P.P.S.

> *"Writing a poem is like catching a fish."*
> —William Stafford

I.

Often in a crowd I feel like I'm in a car wash
but I forgot my car and I'm getting drenched
and broken or worse, I feel like the quarter
on the carpet that no one picks up because
it's not paper money. By now everyone
with anywhere to be has gone there
in their blue Trans Ams and good riddance.
There's only enough room in these rooms for
a few heads wondering how anyone deals with
three score and ten, even a life spent in cozy
American suburbia, only enough room, and
barely enough, for a few hearts willing to feel
the whole unbearable weight of the truth
about themselves. The truth is in my dreams

II.

I am a fish drawn irresistibly
to a wormy hook, and I wake,
kind of flopping around
with a moth on my tongue.
The first time I was in love I thought
I was in the ocean, but really I was
in a bucket, and when I was thrown back
for being too small, I missed the hook
in my mouth, and it was hard
to breathe during my freefall.
Dear Everyone Who Stayed This Long,
I almost forgot to tell you
I once caught a fish that was This Big.
I cooked it up, it fed me, and I saved some for you.

Acknowledgments

Some of these poems have been previously published, as indicated below.

Anti-: "Um"

Atlanta Review: "Turning Yourself into the Wind"

Catch Up: "No One to Ask for Directions"

Diode Poetry Journal: "Wives of the Poets," "Elegy/Litany," and "At the Afterlife Bar and Grill"

The Fiddleback: "Death and Other Dirty Jokes"

Leveler: "Inside the Belly"

The Louisville Review: "Permanent"

The National Poetry Review: "Self-Portrait as a Child's Stick Figure Drawing on a Refrigerator"

New South: "Thaw"

Paddlefish: "Confessions of a Failed Beatnik"

Perspectives: "Psalm on a Theme by Dean Young and a Somewhat Similar Theme by Allen Ginsberg"

Rosebud: "Road Test"

The Scream: "Scotch Tape World"

Valparaiso Poetry Review: "Um"

Verse Daily: "Self-Portrait as a Child's Stick Figure Drawing on a Refrigerator"

Verse Wisconsin: "Psalm on a Theme by Dean Young and a Somewhat Similar Theme by Allen Ginsberg"